D1470256

World Religions

JUDAISM

Ian Graham

Boca Raton Public Library, Boca Raton, FL

WORLD RELIGIONS

BUDDHISM   CHRISTIANITY   HINDUISM   ISLAM   JUDAISM   SIKHISM

Library and Archives Canada Cataloguing in Publication

Graham, Ian, 1953-
      Judaism / Ian Graham.
(World religions)

ISBN 1-55285-656-9

    1. Judaism--Juvenile literature. I. Title. II. Series: World religions (North Vancouver, B.C.)

BM573.G73 2005   j296   C2004-906015-5

Editorial Manager: Joyce Bentley
Project Editor: Lionel Bender
Designer: Richard Johnson
Proofreader: Jennifer Smart
Cover Make-up: Mike Spender, Additional Design
Diagrams and maps: Stefan Chabluk
Picture Researchers: Joanne O'Brien at Circa Photo Library, and Cathy Stastny
Produced by Bender Richardson White, PO Box 266, Uxbridge, UB9 5NX, U.K.

Senior Editor: Sarah Nunn
Text Editors: Peter Harrison
Art Editor: Ben White
Indexer: Peter Harrison

Thanks to Joanne O'Brien at ICOREC, Manchester, U.K. for planning the structure and content of these books. Thanks, too, to Judaism Consultant Rabbi Dr Charles Middleburgh, former Executive Director of the Union of Liberal and Progressive Judaism.

The Publisher acknowledges the financial support of the Government of Canada through the Book Publishing Industry Development Program for our publishing activities.

Printed and bound in China

Picture Acknowledgments
We wish to thank the following individuals and organizations for their help and assistance, and for supplying material in their collections: Circa Photo Library: cover and pages 1, 3, 4, 5 top, 6, 8, 9, 12, 13, 14, 16, 18, 19, 20, 21, 22, 23, 24, 27, 29, 31, 32, 33, 35, 36, 37, 39, 40, 48–49, 50–51, 52–53 (Barrie Searle); 7, 54–55 (William Holtby); 11, 17, 41 (Zbigniew Kosc); 28 (Ged Murray). Corbis Images: pages 10 (Paul Souders); 30 (Richard T. Nowitz); 34 (Archivo Iconografico); 44 (Tom & Dee Ann McCarthy); 45 (Corbis Images Inc.). Topham Photo Library: pages 5 center (Picturepoint); 5 bottom (The ImageWorks/Jeff Greenberg); 15 (Picturepoint); 25 (The ImageWorks/David Wells); 38 (Picturepoint); 42 (Press Association); 43 (The ImageWorks); 46 (The Image Works/Larry Mulverhill), 47 (Press Association/AFPI. The pictures used in this book do not show the actual people named in the case studies in the text.

CONTENTS

Jonathan's Story

Jonathan and his family live in a Jewish neighborhood of New York City, U.S.A. He is 15 years old, and he and his younger sister attend the local high school, where there are many other Jewish children. Jonathan's family are members of a Conservative temple in the center of Manhattan.

"JUDAISM IS AN important part of my life. With my sister and parents, I go to temple every Saturday morning for the Sabbath service. On Friday evenings at home, at sunset, my mother lights the Sabbath candles, we say the blessings over bread and wine, which we then share, and we have a family meal. In the winter, my school allows Jewish children to leave early on Friday afternoons so we can get home well before the Sabbath starts. Throughout the year, and especially for the Jewish New Year, the school also allows us days off to celebrate our festivals.

At school, my friends are of all faiths. We hang out together during the day and in the evenings, and often meet up on Sundays. We play sport, go to the movie theater, or go out for a meal.

At home my family buys and eats only kosher food, but unlike some of my Jewish friends, when we go out to restaurants, we do sometimes eat non-kosher foods. We believe that some traditional Jewish beliefs are no longer relevant to the modern era.

Now that I have had my bar mitzvah and understand more about my faith, my parents are encouraging me to go on a student tour of Israel this summer. I will go with lots of other Jewish teenagers from my temple. The tour will take us to historic Jewish sites in Israel but also, if safe, to the Arab quarter and Christian sites of Jerusalem. We will learn about the similarities between the Jewish, Christian, and Muslim faiths and why each regards Jerusalem as a holy city. I will also visit some distant relatives who used to live in Russia, but now live on a kibbutz near the border with Lebanon.

Later this year my sister will have her bat mitzvah. This will be a joyous occasion when friends and relatives will join my family in the temple to celebrate my sister becoming an adult member of the Jewish community. She will read a passage from the Torah, our holy scripture, and take part of the Sabbath service.

When I grow up, I hope to join my father in his business. I also hope to meet a Jewish girl, get married, and have children. We will bring up our children in the Jewish faith and send them to cheder every Sunday to be taught the traditions and customs of our faith."

Jews across the world

There are around 14 million Jews worldwide. The majority live in the United States of America.

ISRAEL
The Israeli flag hangs from the front of a synagogue in Jerusalem. On the roof of the building is a menorah, a symbol of the faith. Israel is the only country in the world with a predominantly Jewish population.

EUROPE
The interior of a synagogue in Portsmouth, England. The Jewish population of eastern and western European countries has fluctuated over the centuries as successive rulers tolerated or persecuted Jews.

NORTH AMERICA
Jews praying in a small community synagogue. About a century ago, millions of Jews fled persecution in Eastern Europe and emigrated to North America. There are more Jews in the U.S.A. than in Israel.

What Is Judaism?

Judaism is more than just a religion. It is the entire culture, history, and civilization of the Jewish people.

AT ITS CORE, Judaism is a religion, but it is also a way of living and thinking, a body of literature, a society, a musical tradition, a language, and a history that stretches back 4000 years. It is built upon a code of beliefs, laws, and teachings that are set out in the Hebrew Bible and other Jewish religious texts. It is not a remote or purely academic philosophy. Its laws and customs have provided a framework for a practical and spiritual way of life for Jews from the origins of Judaism right up to the present day.

What are the fundamentals of Judaism?

There are three basic principles of faith at the heart of Judaism – God, the Torah,

Was Jesus the Messiah?

Christians believe that Jesus Christ was the Messiah, but Jews do not. Jews believe the Messiah's arrival will bring about the restoration of the Temple in Jerusalem and all its rituals, and will also mark the establishment of God's Kingdom on Earth. Because violence and war have not ended in the 2000 years since Jesus, Jews say that Jesus cannot have been the Messiah.

Men and a teenage boy, wearing all the apparel associated with Jewish worship and prayer, parade a Torah in front of the Western Wall in Jerusalem, Israel.

A menorah, a seven-branched candelabrum, is the traditional symbol of Judaism, recalling the one in the ancient Temple in Jerusalem.

DEBATE - Are religious laws a benefit?

- Yes. They give people guidance on how to live their lives and treat each other. Without rules, some people would think only of themselves.

- No. They were written thousands of years ago and don't apply to the lives people lead today. Slavishly following them, without thought or understanding, teaches people nothing.

and Israel. Firstly, Jews believe there is only one God, the Creator, who is eternal, all-powerful, all-knowing, and loving. Judaism was the first monotheistic religion, the first to teach that there is only one God. Secondly, Jews believe the word of God was revealed directly to the prophet Moses on Mount Sinai and was written down by him as the five books of the Torah (the first five books of the Hebrew Bible). Thirdly, they believe that Israel was granted to the Israelites by God as a Promised Land. Jews further believe that God made a covenant, or agreement, with their ancestors, choosing them to be a "kingdom of priests and a holy people."

Being "chosen" does not mean that Jews believe they are superior. They believe that everyone is created in God's image. It follows from this that all people are created equal, and therefore no person or nation can be superior to any other.

Jews believe that death is part of life. They also believe in the immortality of the soul. The ancient Rabbis believed in a "world to come" inhabited by the righteous after their death.

Judaism believes in the coming of a Messiah. The word "Messiah" comes from the Hebrew word *mashiah*, which means "anointed one." Jewish kings and high priests were anointed with oil when they were crowned, so, in time, "the anointed one" came to mean anyone chosen for a special purpose. The Messiah is therefore the one chosen by God for His purpose. Jews believe the Messiah will unite people and lead the world into a new age of peace, justice, and equal rights for all.

What are the Jewish holy writings?

The most important Jewish holy text is the Hebrew Bible, or *Tanakh*. It is a collection of 39 books divided into three parts – the Torah, the Prophets, and the Writings.

The Torah contains many of the laws that Jews live by, especially the Ten Commandments. It is composed of the Five Books of Moses – Genesis, Exodus, Leviticus, Numbers, and Deuteronomy. These are also known to Christians as the first five books of the Old Testament, or Pentateuch. The traditional Jewish belief is that the Pentateuch was revealed by God directly to Moses. This means that the Torah is changeless, because it is believed to be the word of God, but progressive Judaism teaches that people's circumstances, ideas, and values

A scribe uses a quill pen and ink to make a copy of the Torah.

The Ten Commandments

The Ten Commandments were inscribed on two stone tablets by God and given to Moses.

1. You shall have no other gods before me.

2. You shall not make for yourself graven images, or bow down to them or serve them.

3. You shall not take the name of the Lord your God in vain.

4. Remember the Sabbath day, to keep it holy. Six days you shall labor and do all your work, but the seventh day is a Sabbath to the Lord your God; on it you shall not do any work.

5. Honour your father and mother.

6. You shall not kill.

7. You shall not commit adultery.

8. You shall not steal.

9. You shall not bear false witness against your neighbor.

10. You shall not covet your neighbor's goods or wife .

change as generations come and go. Therefore the interpretation of the Torah changes with the passage of time. Jews sometimes use the word Torah (meaning teaching) to refer to the whole Bible, or even the whole of Jewish teaching in all its forms.

The second section of the Bible is the Prophets. Prophets were people who received God's word directly and so spoke with divine inspiration. They expressed God's will for the people. The Prophets comprises historical texts, speeches, and instruction by the Hebrew prophets. Part of it is a collection of 12 shorter works, known as the Minor Prophets. The final section, the Writings, contains 13 books of poems, songs, historical stories, and wise sayings. The Prophets and Writings also appear in the Christian Old Testament.

How do Jews interpret the Torah?

When Moses was given the Torah, he also received oral explanations of its meaning. These, called the oral Torah, were passed on by word of mouth from Moses to Joshua, his successor as leader of the Israelites, and to the prophets, elders, and Rabbis over the generations.

These oral teachings and traditions were brought together in a single written work called the *Mishnah* (meaning "learning by repetition,") which was further interpreted in a second work called the *Gemara* (completion). The Mishnah and Gemara together are called the Talmud (instruction). The Talmud is nearly 2000 years old, but it is still studied today with the Bible, and still serves as a guide to Jewish law and traditional Jewish life.

What is Jewish Law?

Jewish Law is called *halakhah*. A literal translation would be something like "to travel" or "to follow a path." It shows the correct path to follow through life. Halakhah began with the Torah, the part of the Bible given to Moses and interpreted in the Talmud, but it has evolved and grown since then. It now comprises three elements.

The first is the *mitzvot*. These are the 613 commandments written in the Torah. The Rabbis divided them into 248 positive and 365 negative mitzvot. A positive *mitzvah* (the singular of mitzvot) is a divine instruction to do something – you shall give to charity according to your means, for example. A negative mitzvah is a prohibition, such as, you shall not bear a grudge or, you shall not steal. Some positive and negative mitzvot duplicate each other. The instructions to rest on the Sabbath and not to work on the Sabbath mean the same thing. All of the 613 mitzvot are considered to be equally important and equally sacred, no matter how trivial or mundane they may seem to be.

The second element is composed of laws added later by the Rabbis. And, finally, there are long-standing traditions, customs, and practices that have acquired the status of laws. These later

DEBATE – Should religious laws be followed exactly?

- Yes. Laws handed down by God are not open to interpretation by people, who could, knowingly or unknowingly, change them to suit themselves.

- No. If ancient laws do not apply to modern society, they should be revised or dispensed with altogether.

Judaism puts great importance on education. Here, a girl in cheder (a Sunday morning religious class) learns the Hebrew alphabet.

additions are not considered to be as important or as unchangeable as the divine commands of the Torah.

Do all Jewish laws apply today?

All the laws still apply, but some of them are impossible to observe now, because they relate to activities, situations, or places that no longer exist. These include laws governing sacrifices, or laws that relate to a theocratic state of Israel (governed by priests). The present state of Israel is a secular state, meaning that it is governed by elected politicians. There are also laws that only apply within Israel itself or to certain people. About 270 of the original 613 mitzvot are applicable today to Jews living outside Israel, but only the most Orthodox Jews observe them all. Other, more liberal Jewish groups, observe fewer laws.

What are the similarities between Judaism, Christianity, and Islam?

All three religions, or faiths, originated in the Middle East between 1000 and 3000 years ago. All three are monotheistic, believing in one God. They all share some common traditions, going back to Abraham. All believe God's Word is revealed in their holy book.

They are all ethical religions, concerned that their followers should lead morally correct lives, in accordance with the will of God.

At a yeshiva in Jerusalem, Orthodox Jews immerse themselves in both religious and secular studies.

What Are The Origins Of Judaism?

Judaism is traced back to Abraham, Isaac, and Jacob, known as the Patriarchs, in the ancient lands of the eastern Mediterranean. Its history is one of famine, slavery, war, and invasion.

THE HISTORY OF Judaism begins with a shepherd called Abram, who lived in southern Mesopotamia (modern Iraq) in about 1800 B.C.E. Abram rejected the worshiping of idols, which was common at that time. Instead, he believed that everything in existence was made by a single Creator. God, the Creator, spoke to Abram and offered to make a covenant, or agreement, with him. If Abram would leave his home and go to a new "Promised Land" and if he and his descendants agreed to keep God's laws, then they would create a great nation. Abram accepted. He spent years traveling through Canaan, the

The Sinai Desert in Israel, in which many of the events in early Jewish history took place.

The Seder Plate – a ceremonial dish on which various foods are placed and used at the Passover festival. The foods represent the conditions of the Israelites' slavery in Egypt and their subsequent escape.

Who were the 12 tribes of Israel?

Jacob had 12 sons, named (from first-born to last) Reuben, Simeon, Levi, Judah, Dan, Naphtali, Gad, Asher, Issachar, Zebulun, Joseph, and Benjamin. All except Joseph and Levi founded tribes. Another two tribes were founded by Joseph's sons, Manasseh and Ephraim. These were the 12 tribes of Israel.

region between the River Jordan and the Mediterranean, and the Nile Delta as a shepherd.

Who are the Children of Israel?

Abram had two sons. He had the first, Ishmael, by his wife's maidservant, Hagar. Then, when he was 100 years old, God blessed him with a son, Isaac, by his wife, Sarai. God also changed Abram's name to Abraham, and Sarai's to Sarah.

Isaac had two sons. He called them Jacob and Esau. God changed Jacob's name to Israel, so Jacob's descendants are also known as the Children of Israel, or the Israelites. When a famine struck

Canaan, Jacob and his family left and settled in Egypt. Their descendants lived comfortably in Egypt for several generations until a new Pharaoh turned against them and enslaved them.

To reduce their numbers, the Pharaoh ordered all Israelite boys to be killed at birth. One baby escaped the slaughter by being hidden in a basket at the edge of a river. He was found there by the Pharaoh's daughter, given the name Moses and brought up in the Egyptian royal court. He later discovered he was Hebrew, and when he saw an Egyptian ill-treating a Hebrew slave, he killed the Egyptian and then fled for his life.

Moses became a shepherd in Midian, a land in the northwestern part of the modern Arabian desert. While he was tending his sheep one day, he was amazed to see a burning bush that was not consumed by the flames, and he heard the voice of God commanding him to return to Egypt and free his people.

How did the Israelites escape slavery?

Moses demanded that the Pharaoh let the Israelites go from slavery in Egypt, but the Pharaoh refused. God then sent ten plagues to punish the Egyptians. The tenth plague resulted in the death of the first-born son of every Egyptian family. Before this happened, God warned the Israelites, who smeared lamb's blood on their door-posts so that the Angel of Death would pass over them. The Feast of the Passover (known as *Pesach* in Hebrew) commemorates this.

The Pharaoh finally let the Israelites go, but then sent an army chasing after them. The Israelites' flight from Egypt under the leadership of Moses is known as the Exodus. God parted the waters of the Red Sea to let the Israelites cross, but

The ten plagues of Egypt

1. The River Nile ran red as blood and all the fish died.
2. A plague of frogs.
3. A plague of lice.
4. A plague of flies.
5. A plague of livestock disease.
6. A plague of boils.
7. A plague of hail.
8. A plague of locusts.
9. Darkness descended on the land for three days.
10. The death of the first–born sons of Egypt.

A Roman mosaic in Tiberios, Israel, showing a synagogue and a menorah. The Romans occupied the Holy Land for several hundred years, including the time of Jesus Christ, who was a learned Jew.

Moses carries the tablets of stone on which are written the Ten Commandments. The painting is by the seventeenth-century Dutch painter, Rembrandt.

brought the water tumbling down on the Egyptian army when it tried to follow them. When the Israelites reached Mount Sinai, Moses climbed the mountain alone and there he received the Ten Commandments, written in stone by God.

How was Israel destroyed?

The Israelites crossed the River Jordan into Canaan, the Promised Land, in about 1250 B.C.E. They conquered Canaan under the leadership of Joshua. Ten of the 12 tribes settled in the north. The remaining two tribes, of Judah and Benjamin, settled in the south. At first, they were ruled by Judges, who were military leaders, then Saul became the first King of Israel in about 1020 B.C.E. He was succeeded by David and then Solomon. When Solomon died, the northern tribes rebelled and formed their own kingdom of Israel. The southern tribes of Judah and Benjamin formed the kingdom of Judah.

The northern tribes lost territory to invading neighbors and were deported by the Assyrians until they disappeared altogether. They later became known as the Ten Lost Tribes. The kingdom of Judah survived until the Babylonians invaded in about 587 B.C.E. and took the people away into exile in Babylon, an ancient city in what is now Iraq. The Babylonian Empire was in turn conquered by the Persians, and their empire was conquered by the Greeks under Alexander the Great. The Israelites did not return to their land until about 530 B.C.E. Then, in 63 B.C.E., the Roman

Why are Jews called Jews?

The religion of the kingdom of Judah became known as Judah-ism, or Judaism, and the people who belonged to it became known as Jews. Until then, they had been known as Hebrews.

army invaded and conquered them, renaming the land Palestine. In 70 C.E., the Romans destroyed the holy Jewish Temple in Jerusalem and in 135 C.E. the Jewish people were exiled from the land of Israel.

Every time Israel was invaded, attacked, or conquered, more of the people fled to other lands, taking their religion with them. This spreading of the Jewish people around the world became known as the Diaspora.

What Are The Main Jewish Traditions?

Jewish identity is reinforced by the many rituals and traditions that have been handed down from antiquity. These were especially important to Jews at times when they did not have a homeland to help establish their identity.

RITES OF PASSAGE are ceremonies performed to mark important milestones in life, such as birth, marriage, and death. On the eighth day of life, Jewish boys are ritually circumcized by having the foreskin of the penis removed. This ritual commemorates Abraham's circumcision of himself and his sons, Isaac and Ishmael, to make their covenant with God. There is no equivalent ritual for girls, but a separate ceremony where baby boys and girls are given a Hebrew name is often held.

Marriage and family life are very important to Jews. A marriage ceremony can be held in a synagogue, a Jewish place of worship, but it need not be. Jewish marriage is a civil contract between a man and a woman. Even so, a Rabbi, or Jewish spiritual leader, is normally present and two independent witnesses are essential. During the ceremony, the bride and groom stand under a *chuppah* (canopy) to symbolize their union. The bridegroom places a ring on his bride's finger. Then the *ketubbah* (marriage contract) is read out. This lists the couple's obligations to each other. Blessings are said, then the couple

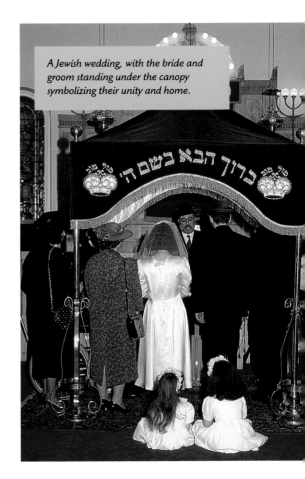

A Jewish wedding, with the bride and groom standing under the canopy symbolizing their unity and home.

drink wine, and the groom breaks a glass under his foot, probably to symbolize the destruction of the ancient Temple in

Orthodox Jews visit the graves of respected Jews in the Valley of Kidron in Jerusalem.

Equality for girls?

In Orthodox Judaism, there is no equivalent to the boy's bar mitzvah for girls. There is a ceremony called *bat chayil* (daughter of strength), when girls read and receive a blessing in the synagogue. In the Conservative and Reform movements, girls may have a bat mitzvah ceremony that is equivalent in every way to a boy's bar mitzvah; Reform Judaism also has a further ceremony at 15 or 16, called a *Kabbalat Torah* (acceptance of the Torah), when participants may conduct the entire service, and give an address affirming their faith.

Jerusalem. Family and friends will then join together to celebrate the marriage.

How do Jews mourn for the dead?

If a parent dies, sons and daughters traditionally tear their clothes over their heart. If another relative dies, the tear is on the right side. In the day or two between death and burial, no one visits the mourners so they can concentrate on the dead. For seven days after the burial, the mourners do not work or do anything for pleasure. Services are held every evening. For 30 days after the death, the mourners do not go to parties or listen to music. Parents continue mourning a dead child for 12 months by reciting the Memorial prayer known as *Kaddish*. On every anniversary of the death, a candle is lit in the home to remember the person, and their name may be mentioned in synagogue on, or near to, the actual anniversary.

What is a Bar Mitzvah?

According to Jewish Law, boys take responsibility for their own actions from the age of 13. At this age, a boy becomes a Bar Mitzvah (son of a Commandment). The equivalent age for girls is 12. A boy's passage into religious adulthood is marked by a bar mitzvah ceremony in the synagogue. The boy reads from the Torah and often gives an explanation in front of a congregation that includes his family and friends. The ceremony is often followed by a celebration that embraces the whole family.

A velvet cover on Torah scrolls shows the Star of David, a symbol of the Jewish faith.

Who is a Jew?

There are two ways to become a Jew. Someone can be born a Jew or they can convert to Judaism. Traditionally, to be born a Jew, a baby must have a Jewish mother. The father may be either Jewish or non-Jewish. The reasoning behind this is probably that the identity of a baby's mother is always known with absolute certainty, but the father's is not always certain. More liberal Jews accept someone as being Jewish if either parent is Jewish and the child is brought up as a Jew. Someone who is born a Jew cannot stop being Jewish. No matter how religious or non-religious they are, and even if they convert to another religion, in Jewish Law they do not stop being Jewish.

How does a non-Jew become a Jew?

To become Jewish, it is not enough to share all the beliefs and practices of Judaism. A non-Jew can become a Jew only by undergoing the formal process of conversion. The first step is to learn the Jewish laws and customs, and start living by them. A Rabbi supervises the convert, who must also attend formal study classes.

The next step is to take an oral or written examination before a *Beit Din* (rabbinical court). If successful, male converts are then circumcized. If they are circumcized already, a symbolic drop of blood is taken. All converts are then immersed in water to symbolize their purification. They usually do it in a purpose-built water-bath, called a *mikveh*, but it could be done in a river or some other natural water. Finally, the convert is given his or her new Jewish name.

Children can be converted to Judaism too. Jewish parents might want to convert adopted children. Mixed faith

(Jewish/non-Jewish) parents might want to convert children who were not born as Jews. Traditional Judaism requires a boy convert to be circumcized and both boys and girls are immersed in a mikveh. Other groups merely hold a naming ceremony. Children can reject the conversion if they wish at the age of 12 (girls) or 13 (boys), when they become "adult" under Jewish Law.

DEBATE – Should infants be converted to Judaism?

• Yes. Being Jewish, and feeling part of the family religion, is a privilege that should not be denied because of age.

• No. The decision should wait until the person is old enough to make up his or her own mind.

Jews visit and pray at the Western Wall in Jerusalem; men and women are separated. The ancient Temple is a site of pilgrimage for Jews all over the world.

What are the branches of Judaism?

There are separate groups within Judaism which have come to different conclusions about what being Jewish means. The core beliefs and customs of Judaism are shared by all Jews, but some Jews believe that the laws and customs can be modified or re-interpreted to reflect changes in society. The main movements within Judaism are Orthodox, Reform, and Liberal (UK and Europe) or Orthodox, Conservative, and Reform (U.S.A.).

Orthodox Jews are the most traditional. They conduct services in Hebrew and observe the laws of the Torah to the letter. Within Orthodoxy, Hassidic Jews are the most traditional. The men wear black coats and hats modeled on clothing from eighteenth-century Poland where the movement began. Lubavitch Hassidism, often known simply as Lubavitch, is an international organization that encourages non-Orthodox Jews to return to observing traditional practices.

The largest organized grouping of Jews in the world is the World Union for Progressive Judaism, to which the large majority of the world's Conservative

Hassidic Jews studying. The men are wearing the black clothing, head coverings, and have uncut hair on the face, that are all typical of Hassidim.

Ethiopia's Jews

There are small groups of Jews in the Middle East, Far East, and Africa who are neither Ashkenazic nor Sephardic. Cut off from mainstream Jewish culture, they developed independently. One of these groups, the Falashas, originated in Ethiopia. They remained Jewish when the rest of the kingdom converted to Christianity in the fourth century. In 1991, 20 000 Falashas were flown from war-torn Ethiopia to Israel.

Is Judaism the same the world over?

Historically, the two main world groupings of Jews are Ashkenazic and Sephardic. Ashkenazi Jews originated in Germany, northern France, and eastern Europe. They are named after the Hebrew word for Germany. About 80 percent of Jews are Ashkenazic, including most American Jews. The Sephardim are the Jews of Spain and Portugal, named after the Hebrew word for Spain. When they were driven out of Spain and Portugal in the fifteenth century, they dispersed into North Africa and parts of southern Europe. The two groups have different languages, customs, and diets, because they were influenced by different cultures.

and Reform synagogues belong. Along with the American Conservative Movement, they comprise more than a third of the world's 14 million Jews. The rest are divided between secular, non-observant Jews, and a number of Orthodox and ultra-Orthodox groups.

The Conservative movement (Reform in the U.K.) is quite traditional in most respects, but Conservative Jews are more relaxed about some of the laws. They do not follow all the dietary laws or those relating to working on the Sabbath.

Reform Judaism (Liberal in the United Kingdom) uses the local language for services as well as Hebrew and allows a more prominent role for women, who can become Rabbis, as they can within Reform Judaism.

An Ethiopian Jewish boy. On his forehead he is wearing a tefillin – a small box containing passages from the Torah.

Do all Jews have the same traditions?

The customs and traditions observed by Jews in different places are very similar. They vary according to whether people are Orthodox, Conservative, or Reform, and how much they have integrated into the surrounding culture. For all Jews, no matter how Orthodox they are, no matter where they are, it is important to remember the past.

The same holidays and customs are kept by Jews both within Israel and in other parts of the world, but there are slight differences in the way they are celebrated. For example, some foods associated with festivals vary according to local crops and produce. Non-Israelis traditionally add an extra day to holidays for historical reasons. This is because each month begins at a new moon and, in times past, the new month did not begin officially until at least two people had seen the first glimmer of light from the new moon. Messengers were then sent out from Jerusalem to let everyone know that the new month had started. Jews who lived within Israel received the news quickly, but those who lived in the furthest and most isolated Jewish communities were the last to hear. As a month could be 29 or 30 days long, they could never be sure which day was the first of a new month until they received the news from the official messengers. So, to be sure that they observed all the required customs at the right times, they celebrated them on both of the possible days.

At an Orthodox Jewish wedding, men and women celebrate separately. Here the bride is seated in the middle of a circle of woman, who dance round her.

Two girls prepare for their bat mitzvahs, with the guidance of a Rabbi. Reform and Liberal Jews allow men and women to participate equally in all Jewish customs and traditions.

Why is the New Year two days long?

Two days are always taken for the holiday of Rosh Hashanah (New Year) by Jews everywhere. The messengers who spread the news that a new month had started were not sent out on New Year's day. As a result, no one knew when the first day of the year had arrived, so, once again, they celebrated and observed religious law on both of the possible days. Even when the calendar changed from one based on observation to one that was calculated mathematically, the tradition of the two-day Rosh Hashanah holiday carried on. Reform Jews observe only one day of Rosh Hashanah.

What language do Jewish people speak?

In ancient times, Jews spoke Hebrew or Aramaic. When they settled in Europe, a mixture of mainly Hebrew and German, called *Yiddish*, was spoken. When European Jews dispersed around the world in the twentieth century, they took Yiddish with them and it is still spoken in many Jewish communities. With the foundation of the state of Israel, Hebrew grew in importance again and it is now the national language of Israel.

A father teaches his children the customs, traditions, prayers, and blessings associated with Hannukah, the Jewish festival of lights.

communities can go to learn more about Judaism. Children can usually attend a religious school, or *cheder* (Hebrew for room), at their synagogue. The classes are held after children finish their normal school day during the week or on a Sunday morning. At cheder, children learn the Hebrew language and study parts of the Torah and Talmud. They also learn about Jewish festivals, customs, and history.

Children attend cheder from about five years old. Some synagogues have a kindergarten for even younger pre-school children. Religious education need not stop on reaching adulthood. Adults who want to continue their religious studies can usually attend Bible study meetings and evening classes at the synagogue. Most synagogues also have a well-stocked library of religious books and Jewish texts that members of the community can study.

Another type of school, the *yeshiva* (academy), offers lessons in both academic subjects and religion. *Yeshivot* (the plural of yeshiva) are mainly attended by the children of ultra-Orthodox Jews who generally prefer single-faith schools, if they are available. Students who want to pursue their religious studies further can attend a university or seminary to take a degree or, perhaps, train as a Rabbi.

How do Jews learn about Judaism?

Learning about Judaism begins in the home. Both parents participate in teaching their children about their faith and culture, but mothers are traditionally the Jewish family's educators. Simply living according to Jewish traditions, which children witness and participate in, goes a long way to instilling in children the customs of Judaism, even without any formal class-based studies.

Synagogues play an important role in education, too. They are not only places of worship, they are also places where members of their local Jewish

Is Judaism featured on the Internet?

Jewish news, articles, and texts of all kinds are now available on the World Wide Web. There are many organizations that, between them, provide a vast database of information about almost any aspect of any branch of Judaism and its beliefs and history. Families can check out Jewish schools and colleges by looking at their websites. There are also sites that enable people to put a question to a Rabbi and have it answered.

Jewish children sing songs and hymns at a summer camp in New York State. In the United States especially, Jewish summer camps are popular and well-attended.

DEBATE - Should Jewish children be taught in separate Jewish schools?

- Yes. Jewish schools enable children to be immersed in the Jewish faith and culture in a way that Jewish lessons in a non-Jewish school can never achieve.

- No. Separating children in single-faith schools makes it more difficult for them to mix with other cultures and learn ways to become part of the community they live in.

How Do Jews Worship?

The synagogue is the center of the Jewish religious community, just as the home is the focus of the family. Both have important roles as places of prayer and reflection.

PRAYERS ARE SAID every day during the week, with special prayers on Sabbaths and festival days. Daily prayers are said three times – in the morning (*Shacharit*), afternoon (*Minchah*), and evening (*Ma'ariv*). Traditionally, men go to their synagogue to pray as often as possible, because they are expected to pray in the company of others. Public worship in a synagogue can only happen when at least ten adults are present. In Orthodox synagogues, this *minyan* (quorum or number) must be all men. In non-Orthodox synagogues, women are included in the minyan.

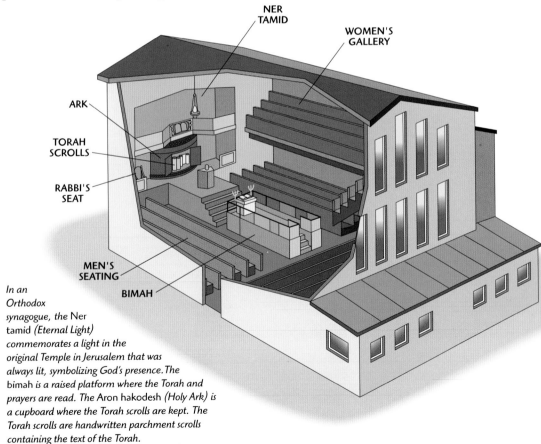

NER TAMID

WOMEN'S GALLERY

ARK

TORAH SCROLLS

RABBI'S SEAT

MEN'S SEATING

BIMAH

In an Orthodox synagogue, the Ner tamid *(Eternal Light) commemorates a light in the original Temple in Jerusalem that was always lit, symbolizing God's presence. The* bimah *is a raised platform where the Torah and prayers are read. The* Aron hakodesh *(Holy Ark) is a cupboard where the Torah scrolls are kept. The Torah scrolls are handwritten parchment scrolls containing the text of the Torah.*

What is a synagogue service like?

When people gather at the synagogue for a service, they sit around, or in front of, a raised platform, or *bimah*, where the Torah and prayers are read. There is a different Torah reading for each week of the year. The Torah is usually read on Mondays, Thursdays, Sabbaths, and some holidays. The Torah is hand-written on parchment scrolls that are normally kept in a cupboard called the *Aron hakodesh* (Holy Ark). The Ark is usually fixed to the wall of the synagogue that faces Jerusalem. When the Torah is read, it must not be touched, partly out of respect and partly to protect the precious parchment from oils and acids on the skin. The person saying the reading uses a pointer to follow the words. To be invited to read from the Torah is a great honor, called an *aliyah*.

In Orthodox synagogues, men and women in the congregation are separated by a screen. In Conservative and Reform synagogues, they are free to sit together. Pre-bar and bat mitzvah children can sit with either parent. Morning service usually begins with a series of blessings, followed by psalms, hymns, and prayers. Prayers are often sung and some synagogues have a cantor who is trained in traditional prayer singing.

The daily prayers are printed together in a book called the *siddur*. After *Shema*, the oldest daily prayer, the most important is *Kaddish*, often called the prayer for the dead, or the mourner's prayer, because it is also said during mourning. In all synagogues, Kaddish is said in its original language, Aramaic.

What does a Rabbi do?

Most synagogues have a Rabbi (teacher), but it is not vital for a synagogue to have one. A Rabbi does not have any more authority to perform rituals than any other male member of the congregation. The Rabbi attends to the religious needs of the community. Orthodox rabbis are always men, while Reform and Liberal Rabbis may be women. Traditionally, a Rabbi is educated in Jewish Law and is therefore able to settle disputes that require interpretation of religious law.

During most synagogue services, the Torah scrolls are taken from the Ark and paraded round the main hall before being taken to the bimah to be read.

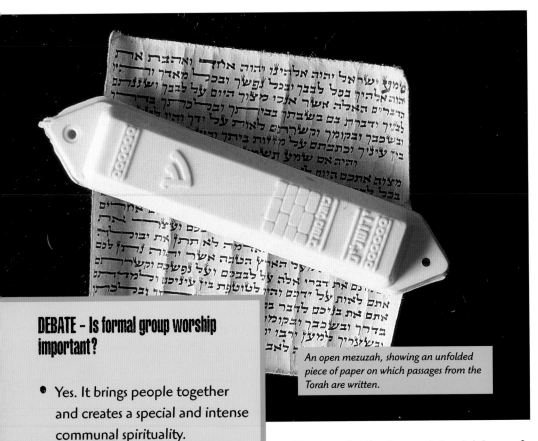

An open mezuzah, showing an unfolded piece of paper on which passages from the Torah are written.

Do Jews worship at home?

Judaism is a way of life, so worship and prayer are not just for special occasions or rituals. Every day is an opportunity for prayer. Worship in the synagogue is an obligation, but prayers are also said at home. Traditionally, Jews pray three times a day at home, just as they do at the synagogue. Prayers are also said before and after each meal. Each type of food has its own blessing. Many of the normal everyday events, such as getting up and going to bed, have their own blessings too.

What marks the doors of Jewish homes?

The front door and main rooms in a Jewish home traditionally have a small box fixed to the right-hand doorpost. Placing them there is a commandment. They are called *mezuzot* (which means doorposts) and they contain two passages from the Torah, handwritten on small pieces of parchment. Their presence is a constant reminder of God's presence in the home, and the family's obligations to God. When someone enters a room, he or she touches the *mezuzah* (the singular of mezuzot) and then kisses the fingers that touched it. Some mezuzah cases are quite plain, but others are very elaborately decorated. When a family moves house, the mezuzot are normally removed and taken to the new house. When they are fixed in place again, there is a dedication ceremony to mark the event.

How strict are Sabbath observances?

It can be difficult for some Orthodox Jews to observe the Sabbath because so many activities are forbidden. It is not permitted to push a baby-buggy or wheelchair outside the home, for example, making it difficult for mothers and disabled people to get to their synagogue. The solution is an *eruv* (meaning to join or mix). When part of a town is marked out as an eruv, the private and public spaces within it are joined together and all of them are treated as one large private space. Within the eruv, people can do things on the Sabbath that are normally forbidden outdoors. Every town in Israel has an eruv, but the first eruv in the UK was not set up until 2002, in part of London.

Covering the head

It is traditional for Jews to cover their head, especially in prayer. Men traditionally wear a small skullcap, from waking to going to bed. Its Hebrew name is a *kippah*; its Yiddish name is *yarmulke*. When men go outdoors, they sometimes wear a proper hat on top of it. Orthodox women who are, or have been, married wear a *sheitel* (a wig) or a scarf. A woman who has never been married does not have to cover her head.

A family celebrates the festival of Sukkot. Each observant Jewish household will build a temporary shelter, a sukkah, and live in it during the festival.

How do Jews keep the Sabbath?

Jews are commanded by God to keep the Sabbath as a special day of rest, worship, reflection, and spiritual enrichment. It echoes the seventh day when God rested from His labors in creating the heavens and the Earth and everything in them. The Jewish Sabbath is Saturday. It is known by its Hebrew name, *Shabbat*.

Traditionally, Jews are not permitted to work on the Sabbath. Not working means more than not going to work. It means not doing anything that involves creating something, just as God refrained from creating anything on the seventh day. Forbidden activities include weaving, sewing, building, making a fire, playing sport, driving a

DEBATE – Should special clothes be worn for worship?

- Yes. They make prayer special, and remind worshippers of the historical reasons for some of the prayers and rituals.
- No. Worship comes from the heart and shouldn't depend on wearing special clothes.

The two candles and challah: symbols related to the start of the Sabbath celebrations.

A Jewish boy binds a tefillin to his arm.

The following morning, the family attends the Shabbat service at the synagogue, which can last from 9.00 a.m. to noon. They return home for a meal, traditionally *cholent* (a type of stew), which can be prepared the day before. The rest of the day is taken up with Torah study, conversation, and leisure.

Shabbat ends at sunset. More blessings are said over candles, wine, and spices to mark the end of the day and the start of a new week.

When do Jews wear a prayer shawl?

Traditional clothes are worn and historic customs are observed during worship. Men wear a *tallit* (shawl). The prayer shawl itself has no meaning, but the fringes or tassels at its corners do. The Torah tells Jews to wear *tzitzit* (fringes) at the corners of garments as a reminder of the Ten Commandments. Originally, twisted threads were added to normal clothes. Later, when Jews moved to other countries with different clothing styles, they adopted the prayer shawl specifically to carry the corner fringes. Orthodox Jewish men also wear a fringed undergarment at all times.

car, cooking, or even carrying something outdoors. Orthodox Jews observe these prohibitions very strictly.

The Sabbath begins at sunset on Friday. The woman of the house lights two candles and says a Sabbath blessing. When the men return from the synagogue, pieces of a fresh loaf of eggy bread, called *challah*, are cut, salted, and eaten, and a glass of wine is shared, with blessings, to honor the beginning of the Sabbath. The man of the house says a prayer called *Kiddush* and the family sits down to dinner. Afterward, grace is said.

What are the bindings Jews wear?

When they pray, Orthodox Jewish men bind a small leather pouch to their forehead and another to their arm with leather straps . These tefillin contain handwritten Torah texts on parchment. Binding them to head and arm is intended to keep God's Word close to the mind and the heart during prayer.

How And What Do Jews Celebrate?

The Jewish year is punctuated with festivals that commemorate important events in Jewish history. All of them are observed strictly by Orthodox Jews, slightly fewer by non-Orthodox Jews. Many of them are associated with special events and experiences, and have special foods.

THE FIVE MAJOR Jewish festivals are *Rosh Hashanah* (Jewish New Year), *Yom Kippur* (Day of Atonement), *Sukkot* (the Feast of Tabernacles), *Pesach* (Passover), and *Shavuot* (the Festival of Weeks). Their observance is required by the Torah. Rosh Hashanah marks the beginning of the year, when Jews examine their lives and accept or renew their responsibilities. It begins a period of ten days of penitence leading up to Yom Kippur, the Day of Atonement.

Yom Kippur is the most sacred day of the year to Jews. It is a day for fasting, confessing one's own sins, expressing regret, and pardoning others. Eating,

drinking, washing, using cosmetics, wearing leather shoes, and sex are all forbidden on Yom Kippur. Traditionally, most of the day is spent in prayer in the

DEBATE – Should one remember the past?

- Yes. It reinforces identity and binds the community by reminding people of their history.
- No. It reawakens old divisions and unhappy memories, and stops people from looking to the future with open minds.

A family sits round the Seder table, about to celebrate the Passover traditions and meal.

A Rabbi blows the shofar. Its most important uses are at New Year services and at the end of the Day of Atonement.

Synagogue services

In Orthodox synagogues, services are held in Hebrew and men primarily "lead" the service. In Conservative and Reform synagogues, about half of the service is in Hebrew and half in the local national language. In Conservative and Reform services, women participate more and there is more community prayer and worship. Orthodox services have a choir and cantor, but no musical accompaniment. An organ is often played during Conservative and Reform services.

synagogue. There, the Ark is covered with a white cloth and worshipers wear white as a symbol of purity. A *shofar* (a ram's horn trumpet) is blown to mark the end of the day.

Sukkot means huts. It refers to the temporary buildings the Jews lived in during the 40 years when they wandered in the desert after the Lord brought them out of Egypt. Jews are commanded to live in a temporary shelter called a *sukkah* for seven days. A sukkah must have three walls and a roof. The roof should be made from something that once grew from the ground, such as reeds or tree branches, and should be laid loosely so that the stars are visible through gaps. During Sukkot, four kinds of plants (a palm branch, three myrtle twigs, two willow branches, and a citron fruit, called *etrog*) are waved in every direction during synagogue services to acknowledge that God is everywhere. Very orthodox Jews will try to sleep in the sukkah.

Pesach celebrates the deliverance of the Israelite people from slavery in Egypt. Its name, meaning Passover, commemorates the time when Israelite homes were passed over during the slaughter of the first-born in Egypt. Unleavened bread, called *matzah*, is eaten on the first night to echo the diet of unleavened bread eaten by the Israelites fleeing from Egypt.

Shavuot was originally a harvest festival, but it also commemorates the giving of the Torah to the Jewish people. It is called the Festival of Weeks because it comes exactly seven weeks after the second day of Passover.

In addition, there are minor festivals, including Hannukah and Purim, and numerous fasts. The minor festivals are not commanded in the Torah, but they commemorate important historical events. Hannukah, which falls around Christmas time, commemorates the recapture of the Temple in 165 B.C.E. by a Jewish army.

A nineteenth–century Jewish calendar.

What is the Jewish calendar?

The Jewish calendar is lunar. Each month begins at a new moon. Most of the world uses the Gregorian calendar, which is solar. A lunar year is about 12.4 solar months long. Over time, the lunar calendar gradually drifts more and more out of agreement with the solar calendar. If no adjustment were made, festivals would occur about 11 days earlier every year. Festivals tied to a season would soon end up in the wrong season. Harvest festivals, for example, could drift back into winter!

To bring the two calendars back into agreement, the years of the Jewish calendar are divided into 19-year cycles and an extra month (Adar II) is added in the third, sixth, eighth, eleventh, fourteenth, seventeenth, and nineteenth years. Further small adjustments are made from year to year to make sure that festivals are kept separate from Sabbaths, so that observing them or preparing for them does not interfere with keeping the Sabbath. All of these adjustments, which vary from year to year, mean that festivals usually fall on different solar dates each year. The solar dates of the various festivals and commemorative days are calculated and printed many years ahead.

Youngsters gather round a table to watch the Hannukah candles, play festive games, and eat festive foods.

The names of the months in the Jewish calendar were originally Hebrew, but during the exile in Babylon, Babylonian names were adopted and they are still used today. The Jewish calendar begins with the month of Nissan, which occurs in March or April, but the year number does not change until the Jewish New Year in the seventh month of Tishri, in September or October. In Babylon, this was the traditional start of the agricultural year.

How are the years numbered?

The year on the Jewish calendar represents the number of years that have passed since creation. This was calculated by the Rabbis by adding up the ages of people listed in the Bible. This gives a creation date of 3761 B.C.E., which must be added to common era dates to convert them to the Jewish year.

Many orthodox Jewish scholars accept that this does not mean that the Universe itself must have been created in precisely 3761 B.C.E. The six "days" of creation could have lasted for any length of time, not necessarily 24 hours each, but, no matter how long it took, they believe that the creation of the Universe was completed by 3761 B.C.E.

Do all holidays have Biblical origins?

New holidays have been added to the Jewish calendar in modern times. Yom Ha-Shoah is a memorial to those who died in the Holocaust. Yom Ha-Zikkaron commemorates those who have died in Israel's wars. Yom Ha-Atzmaut is Israeli Independence Day, the anniversary of the day when the new State of Israel was proclaimed. Finally, Yom Yerushalayim celebrates the reunification of Jerusalem by Israel in 1967.

What are the Jewish dietary laws?

The Torah lays down strict rules for the types of food that Jews may eat and how they should be prepared. Most festivals and celebrations are accompanied by special foods. It is traditional to eat dairy dishes during the festival of Shavuot. Apples or bread dipped in honey are traditional at Rosh Hashanah (New Year). Potato cakes called *latkes* are served during Hannukah, and filled cookies called *hamentaschen* are served during Purim. Traditional meals begin with breaking bread, usually a sweet, eggy bread, called *challah*.

The dietary laws are called *kashrut*, meaning proper or correct. Kosher foods are allowed, *terefah* (ritually unclean) are forbidden. Generally, fruit and vegetables are kosher, but many animals, and their meats, are not. To be kosher, an animal must chew the cud and have hooves that are completely divided in two. So, cows, goats, and sheep are kosher, but pigs are not. Birds neither chew the cud nor have hooves, but not all of them are forbidden. Kosher birds include chicken, turkey, goose, and duck. Only fish with both fins and scales may be eaten, so all shellfish are forbidden. To make shopping easier today, packaged foods in Jewish shops often carry a label or stamp that certifies them as kosher.

These laws date back to the origins of the Jews in the Middle East 4000 years ago. In the hot climate there, scavenging animals, such as pigs, were more likely

A Kosher butcher and delicatessen. In many major cities with a high Jewish population, supermarkets may have special kosher food sections.

Preparing foods for Passover, when no yeast is allowed. Foods for Passover are prepared in kitchens or using dishes specially set aside for the festival, when any substance related to leavened bread is not permitted.

DEBATE – Is it still important to eat "kosher" food today?

- Yes. All Jews can eat in each other's homes and be sure they are eating nothing "forbidden".
- No. All food today is so hygienically prepared that no special certification is necessary.

to carry diseases. Without the luxury of modern refrigerators, eating terefah meats was more likely to result in food poisoning. The Muslim faith, which also originated in the Middle East, has similar dietary laws, called *halal*.

Kosher animals must be killed by *Shehitah* – their throat is cut and blood drained from the body. The meat is soaked or boiled in water, or treated with salt, to draw out even more blood.

Blood is prohibited, because it is traditionally understood to contain the life of the animal.

How is kosher food cooked?

Strict rules govern the preparation of kosher food. In a kosher kitchen, meat and dairy products must be kept apart. They are prepared and cooked separately, using separate sets of crockery and utensils. These are washed in two different sinks, dried with different towels and stored in different cupboards.

Although some foods and dishes are common to all Jews, there is no single Jewish cuisine or style of cooking. Jews who settled in different parts of the world adapted their diet and recipes to make use of local produce and cooking styles.

Has Judaism Changed In Recent Times?

From their origins in Canaan, Jews settled in many countries around the world. Often, they were forced to move because of hostility and persecution. This eventually led to the establishment of the modern State of Israel as a homeland for the world's Jews.

THE WORLDWIDE POPULATION of Jews is approximately 14 million. Most live in the United States and Israel, with about six million in the U.S.A. and four million in Israel, but there are also Jewish communities in Europe, Canada, Latin America, Africa, Asia, Australia, and New Zealand. This dispersion of Jews into different countries around the world is known as the Diaspora.

When and where were Jews persecuted?

In the Middle Ages, rivalry between Christianity and Judaism resulted in long-lasting hostility to Jews throughout Europe. By 1800, most of

What was Kristallnacht?

Nazi violence against Jews exploded on one infamous night, 9 November 1938. In that one night, more than 1000 synagogues, 7500 Jewish-owned businesses and numerous Jewish homes were attacked, and 30 000 Jews were arrested. It was called *Kristallnacht* (Crystal Night) because of the broken glass on German streets.

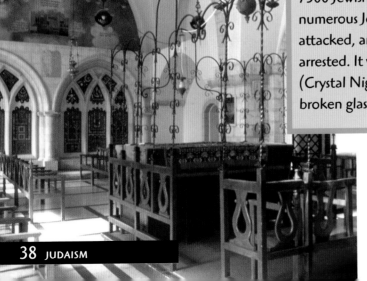

The interior of a synagogue in Jerusalem that was founded in 1492 by Spanish Jews fleeing the Inquisition.

A memorial at Yad Veshem, in Israel, to Jews killed in the Holocaust.

What was the Holocaust?

Nazi Germany initially adopted a policy of deporting Jews to rid itself of them and achieve its aim of racial purity. But as Germany occupied country after country during World War II, deportation was no longer practical. Their "final solution" to the Jewish problem was to exterminate the entire Jewish population of Europe.

Millions of men, women, and children were rounded up and transported to concentration camps in various parts of central and eastern Europe, where they were murdered on an industrial scale. Six million Jews lost their lives in the genocide. An equal number of other "undesirables," including gypsies, mentally handicapped people, homosexuals, and political activists, were exterminated in the same way. This dark episode in twentieth-century history is known as the Holocaust.

Nazi Germany's treatment of the Jews hastened the campaign for the establishment of a Jewish homeland in Israel, a place where the world's Jews hoped to find a safe home, free from fear or oppression.

the world's Jews lived in eastern Europe. They were usually treated as outsiders. There was widespread repression and persecution of Jews in Russia and eastern Europe in the nineteenth century. Massacres known as pogroms led to more than a million leaving for the United States, while others fled to western Europe.

As fascism spread through Europe in the 1930s, anti-Semitism intensified. When the National Socialist (Nazi) party came to power in Germany, they transformed anti-Semitism from religious discrimination to government policy. Jews were officially classified as *Untermenschen* (sub-humans) and forced to identify themselves by wearing a yellow badge. Their rights were restricted, their businesses were attacked and their property was confiscated. Shamefully, few governments came to the aid of the increasingly desperate German Jews.

DEBATE – Does the Holocaust mean there is no God?

- Yes. A loving God would not allow anyone, especially His chosen people, to suffer so.
- No. All people are created by God with free will and they therefore have the capacity to do terrible things as well as good.

How did modern Israel come about?

Small numbers of Jews began to emigrate from Russia and Europe to Palestine in the nineteenth century. At the same time, the Zionist movement campaigned for the establishment of a Jewish homeland in Palestine. Zionism was named after Zion, the hill on which Jerusalem was built.

Britain controlled Palestine and supported the creation of a Jewish state there. There was unrest as Palestinian Arabs resisted the growing numbers of Jewish settlers. The United Nations tried to solve the problem by dividing Palestine into Jewish and Arab territories in 1947. British control ended on 14 May 1948 and Palestinian Jews immediately announced the creation of the State of Israel. The mass emigration of Jews to Israel began. Militant Palestinians, believing their land had been forcefully taken away, began a campaign of terrorism aimed at reclaiming their homeland. The campaign continues to this day and is the basis of the Middle East crisis.

What is a kibbutz?

Long before the State of Israel was established, Jewish settlements in Palestine formed co-operatives called *kibbutzim* (the plural of *kibbutz*), a tradition that still exists.

A kibbutz is formed by a small group of people who pool their resources and work together, mainly on the land. Visitors from other countries are often able to come and live with them for a while. Thousands of young men and women from all over the world have learned about Israel and the Israelis by working on a kibbutz. In return for work, they receive accommodation and food, and sometimes a little money too. Each kibbutz is governed by a committee, and all its property is jointly owned by the kibbutz.

Today in Israel, there are more than 200 kibbutzim, accounting for about 4 percent of Israel's population. The majority of the kibbutzim are still run as agricultural co-operatives, but some manufacture products, or run tourist hotels.

A date plantation on a kibbutz.

Israeli soldiers on guard outside an Austrian hospice on the Via Dolorosa ("Way of Sorrows") in Jerusalem. An Arab walks along the road where Jesus is believed to have carried the cross to his crucifixion. Jerusalem is a holy city for Jews, Muslims, and Christians.

What does Israel mean to Jews?

Anti-Semitism is still widespread throughout the world, but there is not the same pressure on Jews to emigrate to Israel for protection today as there was in the 1930s and 1940s. Even so, Jews all over the world have a strong emotional attachment to Israel. They are generally united in their support for Israel, although there are disagreements and divisions, even within Israel itself. Some Israelis are Orthodox or ultra-Orthodox, others are more liberal and yet others are secular. Some are Ashkenazic, others are Sephardic. Some have lived in Israel since its foundation, while others have arrived much more recently. Some survived the Holocaust, others have never experienced such brutal persecution. There are tensions between some of these groups, who have different ideas about what Israel should be, how it should be governed, how Jews should live, and how Israel should relate to the Palestinians and its neighbors.

Where is Israel?

Israel lies at the eastern end of the Mediterranean Sea. It measures roughly 250 miles from north to south and its greatest width is 75 miles. Its capital city is Jerusalem, which is a holy city for Christians and Muslims, as well as Jews. Some of Israel's borders are disputed with its neighbors because they enclose territory taken in Arab–Israeli wars. The land rises from the coastal strip in the west to hills and mountains overlooking the Great Rift Valley, which runs down the eastern side of the country. The southern part of Israel is a semi-desert region known as the Negev. Israel's flag is white with a blue strip top and bottom, and a blue Star of David (a six-pointed star symbol) in the middle.

How Is Modern Life Challenging Jewish Values?

Today, among most faiths and communities, more marriages end in divorce, young people are more independent, and families are less close-knit. Scientific advances have led to new medical techniques that make it possible to create life in new ways. These and other aspects of modern life challenge those trying to live within Jewish Law.

WHEN A JEWISH marriage breaks down, the couple divorces twice – once to satisfy civil law and a second time according to Jewish Law. To divorce in Jewish Law, the husband obtains a document called a *get* from a Rabbinic court and gives it to his wife in the presence of witnesses. His wife must receive it willingly.

What happens if Jews marry non-Jews?

Traditionally, and still among many ultra-Orthodox Jewish families, parents choose partners for their children, so this

DEBATE – Should human cloning be allowed?

- Yes. Natural human clones (identical twins) are already born without causing any ethical or religious problems.

- No. Artificial human cloning is completely different from the birth of natural twins. It threatens genetic diversity and would make life into a product, creating children without conventional genetic parents.

Intermarriage of Jew and non-Jew is deemed one of the greatest threats to the survival of Judaism.

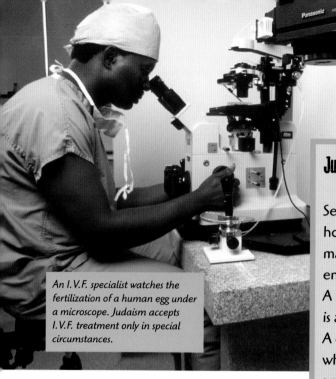
An I.V.F. specialist watches the fertilization of a human egg under a microscope. Judaism accepts I.V.F. treatment only in special circumstances.

problem is unlikely to arise for them. A marriage between a Jew and a non-Jew is not recognized as a marriage under traditional Jewish religious law. In Orthodox Judaism, anyone who "marries out" (marries a non-Jew) may be punished by being cut off from other Jewish people, they cannot enter the World to Come, and their children are not recognized as Jews. Conservative and Reform Jews are more open to mixed-faith marriages.

Do Jews accept assisted conception?

Jews believe that a couple must be focused totally on each other when they conceive a child. New reproductive technologies enable couples to conceive without any intimacy between them. In general, Jewish couples are allowed to use assisted conception, such as in vitro fertilization (I.V.F.) and artificial insemination (A.I.), as long as it involves the use of their own eggs and sperm. Cloning humans, creating people in a laboratory from a single cell, is not permitted.

Are birth control or abortion permitted?

Judaism places great value on life. The use of condoms or other contraceptive methods is forbidden by the commandments, but these only apply to men. So, contraception is not forbidden for women. Abortion is allowed in certain circumstances. A Jewish woman may have an abortion if continuing with the pregnancy would endanger her life. She may also have an abortion if it is necessary for her psychological welfare. A pregnancy that resulted from rape, for example, could be terminated because forcing the woman to carry the unwanted baby would inflict unacceptable mental cruelty on her. Abortion is not allowed for reasons of sex selection or convenience.

Does Judaism accept homosexuality?

Orthodox Jews say the Bible prohibits homosexuality and so it must always be forbidden. That view is not shared in all branches of Judaism. In 1990, the Central Conference of American Rabbis (part of the Reform branch of American Judaism) agreed to ordain gay Rabbis. Then, in 2000, they voted to recognize gay and lesbian relationships. Individual Rabbis had been blessing gay unions in synagogues for some time. They believe that gay people are created by God and so the love they show for each other is just as valid as the love expressed by a straight couple.

Do Jews drink alcohol or take drugs?

Many of the rituals and ceremonies of Judaism are traditionally accompanied by wine, but it is not compulsory to drink wine. Grape juice is just as acceptable as wine, so Jews who do not wish to consume alcohol need not drink wine at all. In general, Jews are forbidden from doing anything harmful to their bodies, so excessive drinking, smoking, or taking harmful drugs is forbidden. Jews are also commanded to obey the law of the land unless it breaks religious law, so taking illegal drugs and driving while under the influence of drink or drugs are not allowed.

What is the role of women in Judaism?

Orthodox Judaism regards women as equal to men, but with different responsibilities. A woman's role is seen as that of wife, mother, and homemaker. Women have a very limited role in synagogue services compared with men. In the Conservative and Reform movements, women enjoy more equality with men and take part in synagogue services. The movements have also been ordaining women as Rabbis since the 1970s, but this is prohibited in Orthodox Judaism.

Judaism permits young people to drink alcohol, providing it is not excessive, and does not go against any of the laws of the land.

Demonstrating for equal rights for women. Orthodox Judaism has been criticized for being male-orientated, but this is not an accurate view.

Are Jews allowed to gamble?

Historically, Jews who indulged in gambling were not allowed to be witnesses in Rabbinic courts. This appears to condemn gambling. Yet, today, some synagogues, especially in the United States, derive income from activities, such as bingo, that involve gambling! The answer is that, in general, gambling is not frowned upon unless it becomes an addiction or leads to problems. In that case, it would break the commandments instructing Jews not to do anything harmful or dangerous to themselves or other people.

What is the Jewish attitude to charity?

Traditionally, Jews are required to give at least one-tenth of their income to charity, but no one is expected to give so much that it makes their own life difficult. Acts of charity of all sorts are known as

DEBATE – Should parents choose marriage partners for their children?

- Yes. Parents have more experience of life, and are able to make a wiser choice of suitable partner.
- No. Individuals know themselves better than anyone else. Also, they need the freedom to make their own choices and their own mistakes.

tzedakah in Hebrew. Tzedakah does not only mean giving money. It can also be satisfied by deeds such as looking after aged parents or other family members, or, for example, by doing voluntary work for the local community.

Is killing ever permitted in Judaism?

Jews believe that nothing must be done to end life prematurely, yet the taking of life is sometimes unavoidable in order to save a life or in time of war. There are also times when it seems kinder to bring life to a close prematurely to end suffering. How does Judaism deal with these issues?

Traditionally, Jews believe that killing is forbidden and peace is better than war. When Jews are attacked, Jewish Law commands them to fight back and, if necessary, kill in self-defence. Murder, deliberate premeditated killing, is a different matter. Murder is always wrong. What about euthanasia (deliberately ending someone's life as an act of mercy)? Is this a permitted killing or is it murder? According to the Torah, there is no distinction between different qualities of life. In general, life must always be preserved. So, a life must run its natural course and therefore euthanasia is wrong. Some more liberal Rabbis have judged that medical treatment or food can be withdrawn from a terminally ill person in a coma and very close to death as long as it is not against the person's previously expressed wishes. It is allowed, because doing so does not interfere with nature. In the same way, a life support machine can be switched off, because doing so merely allows nature to take its course.

Do Jews believe in capital punishment?

In ancient times, when Jews sat in judgement on each other, people were sometimes sentenced to death, but it was

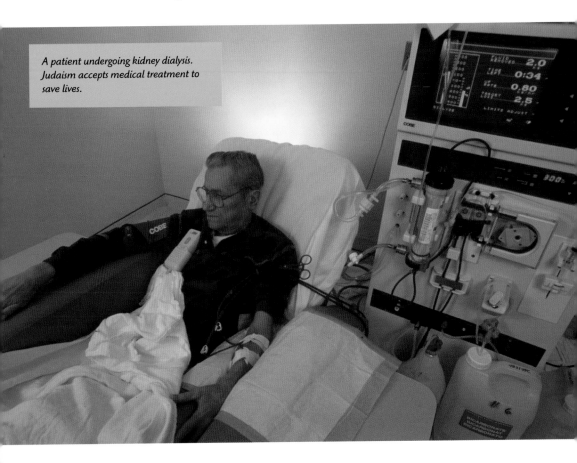

A patient undergoing kidney dialysis. Judaism accepts medical treatment to save lives.

In Jennin, on the West Bank of the River Jordan, Israeli soldiers withdraw from a battle with Palestinians in a refugee camp. Many Jews are uncomfortable with the politics in Israel as they seriously challenge the ethics of Judaism.

very rare. Jews believed that punishments should not be handed out through hatred or revenge, but rather to demonstrate to the community how unacceptable certain crimes were.

Today, Jews live in many different countries and states around the world, with different policies on capital punishment. Jews accept that governments have the right to impose capital punishment in their own legal systems. Many Jews are opposed to capital punishment because it has always been the penalty of last resort for only the most extraordinary and exceptional cases. In addition, if a mistake is made and an innocent person is executed, it is impossible to go back and put things right. For all these reasons, most Jews are opposed to capital punishment.

Debate – Should euthanasia be allowed?

- Yes. If people's quality of life is so poor, through age or illness, that dignity has been lost, they should be allowed to end their life, or have it ended for them.

- No. All life is a precious gift from God that people have no right to end prematurely. Permitting euthanasia might pressure the elderly or terminally ill into allowing their lives to be ended against their wishes.

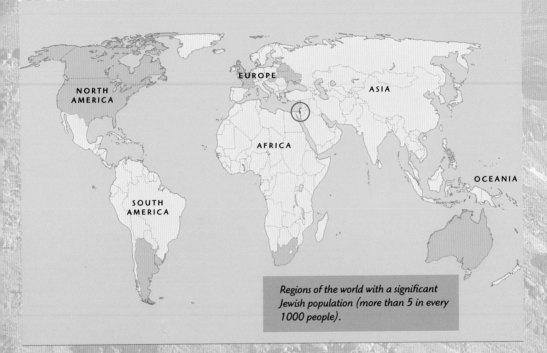

Regions of the world with a significant Jewish population (more than 5 in every 1000 people).

There are around 14 million people worldwide who define themselves as religious Jews. Figures can vary widely depending on whether one takes a religious, cultural, or ethnic definition of being Jewish.

Israel is the only country with a Jewish majority, but more Jews live in the U.S.A. (around 6 million), than in Israel (around 4 million). New York City has an especially large and thriving Jewish community.

The Jewish population of European countries has fluctuated over the centuries as successive rulers tolerated or persecuted Jews. Large-scale Jewish emigration from Europe began in the nineteenth century in response to persecution and poverty especially in Eastern Europe.

In the mid-twentieth century six million Jews, mainly from Eastern Europe, were killed by the Nazi regime, and many more were forced to emigrate. The State of Israel since its formation in 1948 has attracted Jewish immigration from many different parts of the world.

Timeline of Jewish history

NB: most dates before 1000 C.E. are approximate

B.C.E.

2000–1700 Patriarchs: Abraham and Sarah, Isaac and Ishmael

1700–1300 Migration to Egypt followed by slavery

1250 Exodus from Egypt; wandering in the desert, Mount Sinai, Canaan

1000 Kings Saul, David, and Solomon, building of the First Temple

586 First Temple destroyed

586–538 Babylonian exile and return under Persian rule

515 Second Temple completed

311 Alexander the Great conquers Palestine

167 Hasmonean (Maccabean) uprising

146 B.C.E.–400 C.E. Roman rule in Palestine

C.E.

70 Destruction of Jerusalem and the Second Temple

165 Jews exiled from Israel

200 Mishnah (Jewish oral law) compiled

400 Palestinian Talmud edited

550 Babylonian Talmud edited

691 First account of Jews in England

950–1150 Islamic Umayyad dynasty allows Jews to flourish in Spain

1096 Participants in the First Crusade massacre Jews in several Central European cities

1492 Christian reconquest of Spain: expulsion of the Jews

1516, 1555 Jewish ghettos instituted (Venice, Rome)

1730 First synagogue in New York

1881–1924 Russian pogroms against Jews: increasing Jewish emigration to North America

1935–1945 The Holocaust: Nazi persecution of Jews culminating in mass murder

1948 Creation of the State of Israel: opposition from Palestinian population; Jerusalem divided

1967 The Six-Day War: Jerusalem under Israeli control

1978 Camp David Accords

1993 Oslo peace accord

1994 Implementation of Palestinian self-government in Gaza Strip and Jericho area

Jewish calendar and key festivals

The calendar is lunar, with an extra month being added every third year, so that festivals fall at the same time of year. The years are dated from the traditional Jewish dating of the creation of the world (5764 begins in September 2003).

Rosh Hashanah 1 Tishri (September) New Year

Yom Kippur 10 Tishri (September) The Day of Atonement

Sukkot 15–21 Tishri (Sept. / Oct.) In memory of the Israelite wanderings in the desert

Hannukah 25 Kislev–3 Tevet (Dec.) Candles are lit on each of the eight days of the festival

Purim 14 Adar (Feb. / Mar.) The Jewish queen Esther saved her people from a plot to destroy them

Pesach 15–22 Nissan (Mar. / Apr.) The Exodus from Egypt

Shavuot 6–7 Sivan (May / June) The giving of the Torah – the Law – to Moses

The Six Major Faiths

BUDDHISM
Founded
535 B.C.E. in Northern India

Number of followers
Estimated at 360 million

Holy Places
Bodh Gaya, Sarnath, both in northern India

Holy Books
The Tripitaka

Holy Symbol
Eight-spoked wheel

JUDAISM
Founded
In what is now Israel, around 2000 B.C.E.

Number of followers
Around 14 million religious Jews

Holy Places
Jerusalem, especially the Western Wall

Holy Books
The Torah

Holy Symbol
Seven-branched menorah (candle stand)

CHRISTIANITY
Founded
Around 30 B.C.E., Jerusalem

Number of followers
Just under 2000 million

Holy Places
Jerusalem and other sites associated with the life of Jesus

Holy Books
The Bible (Old and New Testament)

Holy Symbol
Cross

HINDUISM
Founded
Developed gradually in prehistoric times

Number of followers
Around 750 million

Holy Places
River Ganges, especially at Varanasi (Benares). Several other places in India

Holy Books
Vedas, Upanishads, Mahabharata, Ramayana

Holy Symbol
Aum

SIKHISM

Founded
Northwest India, 15th century C.E.

Number of followers 22.8 million

Holy Places
There are five important, takhts, or seats of high authority: in Amritsar, Patna Sahib, Anandpur Sahib, Nanded, and Talwandi.

Sacred Scripture
The Guru Granth Sahib

Holy Symbol
The Khanda, the symbol of the Khalsa.

ISLAM

Founded
610 C.E. in Arabia (modern Saudi Arabia)

Number of followers
Over 1000 million

Holy Places
Makkah and Madinah, in Saudi Arabia

Holy Books
The Qur'an

Holy Symbol
Crescent and star

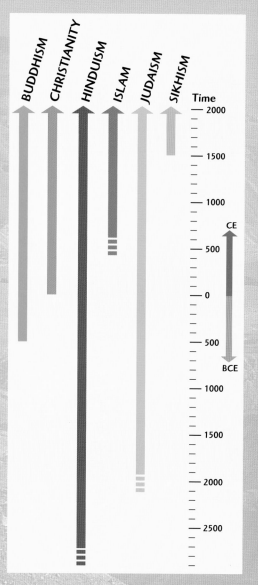

While some faiths can point to a definite time and person for their origin, others can not. For example, Muslims teach that Islam predates Muhammad and goes back to the beginning of the world. Hinduism apparently developed from several different prehistoric religious traditions.

GLOSSARY

anti-Semitism discrimination against Jews.

Ark In a synagogue, the cupboard or curtained alcove where the Torah scrolls are kept. In biblical times, the stone tablets of the Law were carried in a special Ark or chest with carrying poles.

Ashkenazi Jews originating from Germany, France, and eastern Europe.

bar mitzvah A ceremony marking a Jewish boy's thirteenth birthday, when he becomes responsible for his own actions under Jewish religious law.

bat mitzvah A girl's coming of age, at 12 years old, celebrated in many Jewish communities.

Bible The Bible used by Jews corresponds to the Old Testament in the Christian Bible. *See* Tanakh.

bimah A raised platform in a synagogue where the Torah is read.

canon A collection of texts which has been agreed as forming the scriptures.

commandments 613 commandments can be found in the Torah; the passage known as the Ten Commandments summarizes them. *See* mitzvah.

cheder A part-time religious school for children, usually held at a synagogue.

chuppah The canopy a Jewish couple stand under during their marriage ceremony.

Conservative A movement in Judaism that does not require its followers to be as strict as Orthodox Jews.

diaspora The dispersion of Jews from Israel to other countries.

eruv A public space treated as private space to make it easier for Orthodox Jews to get to their synagogues on the Sabbath without breaking commandments.

Exodus The release of the Hebrew people from captivity in Egypt and their journey to the Promised Land, as described in the Bible, the book of Exodus.

Gemara Another term for the Mishnah and the Talmud.

get A document that must be handed from a husband to his wife to divorce under Jewish religious law.

halakhah Jewish religious law.

Hassidism An ultra-traditional form of Orthodox Judaism that originated in Poland.

Holocaust The racial killing in Europe in the 1940s by Nazi Germany in which approximately six million Jewish men, women, and children were murdered.

kashrut The Jewish dietary laws.

ketubbah The marriage contract that lists a husband's and wife's obligations to each other.

kibbutz A co-operative of mainly agricultural workers in Palestine and, later, Israel who live together and share their resources.

kosher Food allowed to be eaten under Jewish religious law.

Magen David The six-pointed star symbol also known as the Shield or Star of David.

menorah A lampstand or candelabrum. The traditional symbol of Judaism is a seven-branched menorah recalling the candelabrum in the Temple. At the festival of Hannukah a nine-branched menorah is lit.

Messiah The person who Jews believe God will send into the world to free them.

mezuzah A small box containing Torah passages on pieces of parchment, fixed to the door-post in a Jewish home.

mikveh A ritual bath used for spiritual cleansing.

minyan The quorum, or minimum number of people, who must be present for public worship in a synagogue.

Mishnah The written form of oral explanations of the Torah and other teachings, which, together with the Gemara, forms the Talmud.

mitzvah A commandment, plural mitzvot.

Oral Torah Explanations of the meaning of the written Torah given to Moses when he received the written Torah.

Orthodox Traditional Judaism (or other faith) which requires strict observance of commandments and customs.

Pentateuch The first five books of the Christian and Hebrew Bibles, known to Jews as the Torah.

prophet Someone who speaks with Divine inspiration.

Prophets The second section of the Hebrew Bible.

Psalm A sacred song.

Rabbi A teacher educated in Jewish religious law, based at a synagogue, who attends to the religious and other needs of the Jewish community.

Reform A branch of Judaism that believes in updating and reinterpreting Jewish religious laws for life in the modern world, known as the Liberal movement in the United Kingdom.

Rosh Hashanah The Jewish New year. It is followed by the "Ten Days of Penitence," leading up to Yom Kippur.

Sabbath English version of the Hebrew word Shabbat. *See* Shabbat.

Sephardi Jews originating from Spain and Portugal.

Shabbat The Jewish Sabbath, Saturday, the seventh day of the week set aside for celebration and relaxation, when no work is done.

shehitah A ritual method for killing animals to produce kosher meat for eating.

Shema The first and most important words of the Torah, enjoining wholehearted worship of the one God. Named after the first word, "Shema," meaning "Hear" in Hebrew.

siddur The Jewish prayer book.

sukkah A temporary shelter made for the festival of Sukkot.

synagogue Jewish house of prayer, study, and community.

tallit A prayer shawl.

Talmud Writings composed of the Mishnah and the Gemara that are studied and used to determine the meaning of the Torah.

Tanakh The Hebrew Bible.

tefillin Two small leather pouches of Torah parchments worn on the head and arm by Orthodox Jews during morning prayers.

Temple Two temples were built in Jerusalem, the first by Solomon around 950 B.C.E., destroyed by the Babylonian in 585; the second by returning exiles 520-515 B.C.E., destroyed by the Romans in 70 C.E. A number of Conservative and Reform congregations refer to their synagogue as a Temple.

Ten Commandments Ten of God's instructions given to Moses on Mount Sinai on tablets of stone.

terefah Food not allowed to be eaten under Jewish religious law.

Torah The first five books of the Hebrew Bible, revealed to Moses on Mount Sinai, and also known as the written Torah.

tzitzit Fringes on the corners of the tallit (prayer shawl).

Western Wall The only remaining section of the Second Temple in Jerusalem, destroyed by the Romans. An important place of pilgrimage and prayer for Jews.

Writings The third and last part of the Hebrew Bible.

yarmulke A small skull-cap worn by some Jews, also known by its Hebrew name of kippah.

yeshiva A Jewish school that offers both secular and religious classes.

Yiddish A language spoken by Jews from Europe, mainly a mixture of Hebrew and German.

Yom Kippur The Jewish Day of Atonement.

Zion The hill on which Jerusalem was built.

Zionism The movement, named after Zion, that campaigned for the establishment of a Jewish homeland in Palestine.

FURTHER INFORMATION

BOOKS

Nachum Amsel, *The Jewish Encyclopedia of Moral and Ethical Issues*, Jason Aronson, 1997
A clearly-written series of essays on issues such as money, sex, honesty, advertising, war and many others, from the standpoint of Jewish tradition. Highly recommended.

Nicholas De Lange, *An Introduction to Judaism*, Cambridge University Press, 2000
A clear account for the general reader of both the history and the present-day practice of Judaism, with tables and maps, a full glossary, chronology, bibliography and index.

Norman Solomon, *Judaism : a very short introduction*, Oxford University Press, 1996
A simple introduction which includes modern concerns and debates, such as the impact of the Holocaust, the establishment of the State of Israel, the status of women, and medical and commercial ethics.

WEBSITES

Judaism.about.com
Provides links to pages on all aspects of Judaism for both Jews and non-Jews.

Learn.jtsa.edu
Site designed for home learning at all levels, provided by the Jewish Theological Seminary of America.

www.torah.org
Education site by Project Genesis, rooted in Conservative Judaism, but aiming to be acceptable to all traditions.

www.jewfaq.org
The Judaism 101 site, by Tracey Rich. A huge amount of information, very clearly organized, with an indication of "basic, intermediate, or advanced" in the page listings. Very useful and comprehensive glossary page. The author does not claim authority, but is a "traditional, observant Jew who has put in a lot of research."

Wupj.org
World Union for Progressive Judaism site, giving an overview of what is distinctive about Progressive Judaism.

www.cjnews.com/default.asp
Home page of *Canadian Jewish News*, Canada's largest Jewish newspaper with links to many Jewish websites and organizations.

ORGANIZATIONS

World Jewish Congress
501 Madison Avenue – 7th Floor
New York, NY, 10022
website: www.wjc.org.il
Amongst other information, gives good concise data about Jewish communities worldwide.

Congress of Secular Jewish Organizations
320 Claymore Blvd
Richamond Heights
OH, 44143
website: www.csjo.org

INDEX